Thanks to;

My husband, Bartley, and our daughters Nuala, Sarah and Maeve for their love and support.
The directors and staff of the Finn Valley Voice for their advice and encouragement.
The readers of the Finn Valley Voice, and especially of the Arched Window, for their encouragement and support.
The members of the Errigal Writers, Letterkenny, for their guidance and critical insight over the years.
Everyone at Donegal County Library, for their support with the research for this book, in particular Liam Ronayne and Frances Crampsie.
Eoghan Holland, design and layout.
Pauline Holland, additional research.
And everyone else who has helped in any way.

And special thanks to:-

The Arts Council of Ireland and Michelle Hoctor.

The John Hewitt Society and Tony Kennedy,
www.johnhewitt.org

The Best of
William Allingham

Edited by
Celine McGlynn.

Voice Books Ltd.

Published 2003 by Voice Books Ltd, Ballybofey, Co Donegal, Ireland

ISBN 0 - 9539265 - 2 - 4

www.voicebooks.net

Selection and Arrangement Copyright Voice Books Ltd.
This Edition published 2003

All rights reserved. No part of this publication may be reproduced, stored in a retrieval system, in any form or by any means, without written prior permission from Voice Books Ltd.

This book is sold subject to the condition that it shall not, by way of trade or otherwise, be lent, re-sold, hired out or otherwise circulated without the publisher's prior consent in any form of binding or cover other than that in which it is published and without a similar condition including this condition being imposed on the subsequent purchaser.

Foreword

William Allingham (1824 – 1889) was Ireland's greatest poet before the
advent of W.B. Yeats, and he remains Donegal's greatest poet to this
day. That alone would be a sufficient reason for this introduction to
his greatest works, the first of our new century.
But there are further, more compelling reasons. It is 150 years
since the publication of his most illustrious work, "Day and Night Songs" and
the anniversary deserves to be marked. It is also nearly forty years since the
last Allingham collection appeared in the Arts Council's Series of Irish
Authors, and it is increasingly difficult for anyone with an interest in
the poet to find his work. As a result, his reputation has been
eclipsed, and he is widely thought of as the author of just three poems,
rather than a lifelong body of work in widely-varying styles.
Those three poems, "The Fairies," "Farewell to Belashanny," and "Four
Ducks on a Pond," are of such arresting quality that they remain in the
mind of anyone who comes across them. And they are but three, of many
dozens of the same quality – hence, again, this book.
In selecting pieces which would both reflect the best of William
Allingham and offer the reader a broad-based introduction to his work, I
had the advantage that W.B. Yeats himself had already selected what he
considered to be the sixteen greatest Allingham poems back in 1905. All
sixteen are included here.
Allingham's longer works present a more difficult choice, but no
collection would be complete without pieces from his verse novel,
"Laurence Bloomfield in Ireland," and from "The Music Master," the work
in which the man who was the poet shines through the most.
I include also the beautiful pre-Raphaelite woodcuts of the Dalziel brothers
after drawings by Rossetti, Millais and Arthur Hughes which Allingham used
to illustrate "Day and Night Songs".
Ulster poet John Hewitt's foreword to the 1967 Arts Council collection
has never been bettered, either as an account of Allingham's life or as
a critical assessment of his work, and I am grateful for the opportunity
to include it here.
Finally, knowing that cultural shifts and changes always make certain
poems more relevant, approachable, or simply more enjoyable to new
readers generations on, I have tried to match what Allingham has to
offer to the wants of new readers by starting, and finishing, with a few
personal favourites.

Celine McGlynn, Ballybofey 2003

Contents

"Crossing the Style"

Introduction by John Hewitt

This introduction was originally written for "The Poems of William Allingham" published for the Irish Arts Council by Dolmen Press in 1967 as part of the "Series of Irish Authors." We are grateful to the Arts Council and the John Hewitt Society for permission to use it here.

William Allingham wrote The Winding Banks of Erne", "Up the Airy Mountain", and "Four Ducks on a Pond", that much we all know from our schooldays; and to be held in his people's memory for the sake of three well loved poems is not a bad fate for any Irish poet beyond Moore and Yeats. But Allingham expected and deserved something more.

The English literary historians have been grudging and badly informed in their references to him, and the Irish have lodged no large claim. As he came from Ireland, in spite of his long stay and the breadth of his friendliness, to the English he has always seemed an outsider. Since he came of Planter stock and spent so long away, by the Irish he has been considered an expatriate, although they allow him his little corner in the Fairy Twilight.

He has never been fully admitted into the body of English literature like Swift, Goldsmith or Joyce. Other Irish writers such as Ferguson, Mangan and Carleton, have suffered a similar sentence; but their names are well established at home and their nationality is never in question. Allingham"s bad luck has been due to our laziness and lack of curiosity as readers, content to leave his books unexplored, taking him as a man of three poems only. The English seldom permit him more than two. His bad luck still dogs him. The concise Oxford Dictionary of Quotations and The Penguin Dictionary of Quotations both remember "The Airy Mountain" and "Four Ducks", and both get the date of his birth wrong.

William Allingham was born at Ballyshannon, County Donegal, on 19th March 1824. His family had come over in Elizabeth's time. His father was a bustling, well-doing merchant with five or six little ships switching cargoes of timber and slates between Canada and the Baltic, once in a while, carrying Irish emigrants to the United States. He was later manager of the local branch of the Provincial Bank and owned some, and rented a little more, land near the town.

William's mother died when he was nine, the eldest of five. After going to a local school where only Latin was taught, in 1837 he was sent as a boarder to another at Killeshandra, County Cavan, where he was miserable and learnt little. At fourteen his father found him a desk at the Bank. The next eight years he worked in branches at Armagh, Strabane, Enniskillen, as well as at home. It was during this period that he made the first of his many visits to London, in the summer of 1843 where he was "all by himself and knew nobody in particular".

A vacancy occurred in the Customs Service in 1846, and William was despatched to Belfast for two months" training, where he preached Tennyson, the new poet, to his fellow clerks, returning as Principal Coast Officer in the town of Donegal at a salary of £80 per annum. The next year he went over to London for the second time, seeing a good deal of Leigh Hunt, with whom he had been corresponding. In July 1849 he was promoted to a post at Ramsey in the Isle of Man, staying there till November. This year's London holiday brought him the friendship of Coventry Patmore, and the following year his first book of poems came out, dedicated to Leigh Hunt.

Within the next three years he had, on his London visits, become friendly with Carlyle, Tennyson and Rossetti, finding the artists and writers associated with the new unconventional Pre–Raphaelite Brotherhood especially congenial. He had also made his first Continental journey, to Belgium. Moved to the Coleraine customs Office, in February 1854 he quit the Service to try his fortune as a freelance writer in London. Homesick after a few months, he had the right wires pulled and was reinstated, this time at New Ross, the break having cost him some promotion. Early in 1855 he was able to exchange with an officer at Ballyshannon, and there he remained until 1862, keeping up with his annual London visits and his friends, and, farther afield, seeing something of Paris, Switzerland, Northern Italy, Holland and Germany.

In March 1863, when he was 39, after a brief exchange from Ballyshannon to the London Docks which ended in a nervous breakdown and a spell back at home to recover, he secured a transfer to Lymington, Hampshire.

At home in Ballyshannon, outside his professional work and his voluminous spare–time reading and writing, he never missed a Fair Day, was a frequent visitor at the infirmary, the national school, and the court house. He sang at parties, walked intensively, knowing every cottage and its folk for twenty miles round, swam, rode and skated enthusiastically, in season. But a humanitarian, he never went hunting, shooting or fishing. Although brought up in the Church of Ireland, by conviction now a deist, on occasion he went to Mass, once accompanied a Lock Derg Pilgrimage, and was friendly with the Catholic

Bishop of Raphoe. He fell in love with a cousin and fell out again, grumbled about the isolation of his position and fretted at the lack of intellectual companionship.

During these years, apart from his London meetings, he kept up a wide correspondence with his friends, chief among them Rossetti and Henry Sutton, a young poet journalist in Nottingham. He had been sending his verses to the magazines, had revised, added to and republished the poems of his 1850 volume which had sold only 43 copies although privately praised by Tennyson. For Day and Night Songs, his 1855 volume, he persuaded his PRB friends, Rossetti, Millais and Arthur Hughes to provide nine illustrations. The wood engravings made by the celebrated Dalziel brothers after the artists' drawings, form a land–mark in English Book Illustration; and Allingham used them again whenever opportunity arose. It was in some of these poems that he utilised the refrain, or line repeated at regular intervals, a device which he may well have picked up from the Border Ballads that he loved so much; a device popular with Rossetti and even more with Morris. But who among them in that group was first to rediscover it, is a nice point. At any rate, Rossetti made his most famous illustration for "The Maids of Elsin Mere" in 1854, in which poem the refrain

"Years ago and years ago:
And the tall reeds sigh as the wind doth blow",

Sounded a note that Yeats found and played magnificent variations on, in the years ahead.

Allingham's excellent and now utterly neglected essay on "Irish Ballad Singers and Street Ballads" was written in 1851, and shortly after, he tried his hand at the genre, picking up folksongs from the country people and either adapting or expanding what words he could overhear, or finding fresh words, if he had caught none, sympathetic to the mood of the melody. These artefacts he sent to Dublin to be printed, anonymously, in the format of the street singers' broadsheets on long strips of tinted paper, ("3 yards of songs"), with appropriate woodcut decorations top and bottom, out of the printer's stock of blocks. When the bundles came back, he gave the individual ballads away or had them sold as the genuine ha'penny ballads were sold at fairs and markets. Then, as object and reward of the exercise, he could hear them sung back to him, passing cottage doors, by folk who had no notion of the author of the words at all. In a letter to Sutton, 17 June 1852, he wrote "In the meantime, I have for some part of my verse, a little audience such as few poets can boast of and to whom Tennyson would, likely, seem to be the name of a town". Although he contrived no more than a fistful of songs in this manner, he pioneered a mode and a technique which has had its lasting triumphs at the hands of Yeats, Colum and Joseph Campbell.

A far more significant achievement spired out of these years also, for, late in 1862, while still at Ballyshannon, he started to serialise his Laurence Bloomfield in Ireland in Fraser's Magazine. Begun a couple of years before, this was the story of a progressive young landlord and his relations with his fellow landlords and their agents, and the oppressed tenantry, involving bailiffs, evictions, Ribbonmen, informers and police, and offering a humane solution to the injustice and class antagonism. In appropriate places he made use of his own observations and the descriptions drawn from his fine earlier essays, the already mentioned "Irish Ballad Singers" and the scarcely less important "The Midsummer Fire", the verbal parallels illuminating both the prose and the verse. By far his longest poem, almost five thousand lines, Laurence Bloomfield was published in book form in 1864. Gladstone quoted from it in the House of Commons, invited the poet to breakfast, and, on Palmerston's recommendation, Allingham received a Civil List pension of £60 per annum. After reading it, Ivan Turgenev, the great Russian novelist, declared to a friend of the poet, "I never understood Ireland before;" Laurence Bloomfield, coming as it did in the years immediately before Allingham's leaving Ireland, may be considered as a watershed; as if, before taking up a new life, he had concentrated his strongest feelings and most telling experiences of his native country into a coherent statement, realising himself in the act. Hence forward, he could move more easily among strangers, with a clarified mind.

Stationed at Lymington, he was within reasonable distance of London, and he spent many weekends in the capital, staying with Burne Jones and his wife: there were also satisfactions closer to hand, the New Forest, later subject for one of his "Rambles", and the Isle of Wright where Tennyson lived, at Farringford.

In 1865 his "Fifty Modern Poems" came out. He went over to Dublin to lecture on "Poetry", staying with Samuel Ferguson, and on to Ballyshannon where his father was not well. Then, in October 1866, he returned for his father's funeral, his last trip home. From then on he was to see a good deal of England, Scotland and Wales, and visit France, which was to provide the material for his serious and intelligently discursive prose Rambles by Patricius Walker (1873): but Ireland was never rooted out of his heart, and slipped back to consciousness when he talked to Highland crofters, to Welsh hill–farmers, or read "the sign–boards of shops and market booths; in Liverpool.

Through Carlyle's influence, he resigned from the Customs Service in 1870, to become sub–editor of Fraser's Magazine, and four years later, Carlyle again the arranger, he succeeded J.A. Froude, the historian, in the editor's chair, a position he held for five years. This same year he married Helen Paterson, a water–colourist, highly thought of by Ruskin and whose cosy portrait of Carlyle at home is now in the Scottish National Portrait Gallery. She was then twenty–six to his fifty, when they set up house in Chelsea. Beside the afore–mentioned Rambles, he also edited "a choice selection of the best British Ballads" (1864), as well as the comprehensive Songs Ballads and Stories (1877), which in its 328 page gathered the bulk of his best verse, but not Laurence Bloomfield. Here too, "The Music Maker, a Love Story" appeared again, the much revised sentimental narrative poem which Patmore had considered "the most touching poem I know", and which Rossetti thought "just too noble", over twenty years before.

In 1881, Allingham moved with his family to Witley, Surrey, where he was visited by Morris and Burne Jones. Six years later his Civil List pension was raised to £100, and in a couple of years, to make easier the children's schooling, he moved to Hampstead, where, after a period of illness, partially as a result of a fall from his horse, he died on 18th November 1889. His body was cremated at Woking and his ashes buried in the churchyard at Ballyshannon.

While living at Witley, he had published Ashy Manor (1882), his only play, a drama of the English Civil War in blank verse and prose. His last years were chiefly occupied in writing the first part of an autobiographical sketch and in preparing his diary for publication, and in sorting out his poems into a series of six volumes: most of these he was able to see through the press; and these, with the posthumous volumes, in effect, form his collected edition.

Allingham's widow, indefatigable in discharging her responsibilities and laying us under her debt, collected his prose in three volumes (1893), edited his Diary (1907), and a selection of Letters received by him (1911). Birkbeck Hill had edited D.G. Rossetti's Letters to Allingham in 1987. Helen Allingham finally made a selection of the verse for Macmillan's Golden Treasury series in 1912. She herself died in 1926, and now none of Allingham's own or the associated volumes is in print.

William Allingham had been intimate with Carlyle, Tennyson, Rossetti and Burne Jones, and good friends with Emerson, Dickens, Robert and Elizabeth Browning; he had talked with Ouida and Henry James, and had called on Thackeray in Paris; he had heard Jenny Lind sing, Cardinal Wiseman and Professor Huxley lecture; he had seen Tom Sayers box and Charles Macready act, had briefed Monchkton Milnes for a House of Commons debate in Irish education; he had been photographed by the famous Mrs. Cameron and had had his bust exhibited in the Royal Academy. Although primarily a man of letters, he was keenly interested in painting, architecture, music, and in the scientific theories of his time. In the depth and range of his intellectual and aesthetic experience he had lived a much richer life than any of his Irish contemporaries.

Opponent of hereditary privilege – he proposed the institution of life–peerages – and a severe critic of visual squalor and social injustice, he had grasped for himself the nature of capitalist credit and finance with its recurring crises. He suggested the nationalisation of all transport, but was never quite a socialist in spite of his wide arcs of agreement with William Morris, wanting 'reforms and thorough–going ones, but not at the hands of atheists or anarchists'. His anti–Imperialism, as we should now call it, was evidenced by his attitude to Indian freedom, and by his sonnet on the Afghan War. In all this and in his support for Irish peasant proprietorship – "Politics or no Politics, I would give the waste lands of Ireland into toilful Irish hands" – he stands squarely in the great nineteenth century radical tradition of Ruskin and Morris; compared with him, all but a very few of the eminent literary men of the period must appear politically naïve and blandly unaware of the nature and dynamics of their society.

This was William Allingham the man. What can fairly be claimed for William Allingham the poet.

A scrupulous artist, meticulous in revision, he could tell a clear story, short or long, in stanzas, in octosylables, or in ballad measure; he could present a dramatic dialogue or analyse a complex character in blank verse; he could express a witty or savage opinion in a pointed quatrian or a memorable distich; he could experiment in the Warwickshire dialect, use the Anglo–Irish vernacular with discretion for lyrical purposes, and essay the old alliterative or unrhymed classical metres; he could round off a sonnet with originality of form; sketch a brisk satirical portrait, and Irish landscape or rural event in resonant couplets; discover a compelling phrase or image for the swiftly changing face of his native western sky or the alternating moods of the sea; evoke the detail of the blossoming hedge–foot; write the finest large–scale Irish political poem in our literature; find lilting rhymes for the fancies of child, and weave the tatters of an old song into a shapely melody.

Measure him against Ferguson and Mangan at their best, and while he may not possess the grave authority, the prosodic resilience, and the imaginative nobility of the former, nor the bold colour, the rhythmic vitality and romantic abundance of the latter, he must be judged to have been technically the most accomplished and emotionally the most sensitive of the three leading Irish poets of the last century.

(VI)

One other matter remains briefly to be considered: Allingham's relationship to his native country.

Although an active person, he was certainly, while he lived at Ballyshannon, a victim of depression. The place could not provide the kind of existence which he felt he needed for his full development as man and writer. Hence the yearly rush across the water; hence, too the attempts to escape.

Born into the Protestant minority, in addition to the cultural isolation, he found himself, by his unorthodox theological and political ideas, driven to become even more alone within that minority. His politics might have served as a bridge to the majority, but already he found that not many of them "would readily trust a Protestant patriot, save in the belief of his readiness to join the true Church, when the proper time should arrive" (1851). This identification of nationality with religion he found irksome but pertinent; "I love Ireland: were she only not Catholic? But would she be Ireland otherwise?"

Consequently he looked back to the days before the Union, when Dublin was, in truth, a capital city, and the Protestant ascendancy, with its Patriot–Parliament, "was" the nation, and felt some identification with the "cultivated Irishmen" of that period. But the subsequent history of the country from the Act of Union to the collapse of the Young Irelanders bred a doubt in his mind of the possibility of a valid National Being; so, for himself and for those like him, "Ireland had ceased to be a country and England was not theirs".

Among the English, when he had made good his escape, this condition persisted. Tennyson and he were continually arguing about Ireland, and once he had to face the charge "You don't care a pin about the grand Empire of England. You ought to be proud surely to be part of it. There you are, with an English name, English in every way, but you happened to be born in Ireland, therefore you are for it". There is no doubt that he found his life as a literary man in London more satisfying than as a scribbling Customs Officer in a small western seaport; but the fact of birth remained. 'It has always been supposed that some countries have, so to speak, a peculiar magnetic affection for the souls of their children, and I found plenty or reason, in the conduct of my neighbours as well as my own consciousness, to count Ireland one of these well–beloved mother–lands;.

Above all, when he thought of himself as a poet, he was immediately aware of a particular need and ambition. Writing to Ferguson, he confessed "the thought is dear to me of distinctly connecting my name as a Poet with that of the Old Country". But the critics persisted in denying him that honour. Because of his most popular verses, his name was consistently linked, not with Ireland, but with his native town, a view which Yeats held and enunciated at

Allingham's chagrin. So, in his diary for Tuesday 18th September 1888, he wrote, "Miss Tynan sends me criticisms from Providence Journal – "The Poet of Ballyshannon", (non–national, how sad!).

The unjust sentence has been allowed to stand too long. It is surely time that we extended an unequivocal salute to one of the best of Ireland's poets and to one of the most civilised of Irishmen.

"Milly"

1

LET ME SING OF WHAT I KNOW

A wild west Coast, a little Town,
Where little Folk go up and down,
Tides flow and winds blow:
Night and Tempest and the Sea,
Human Will and Human Fate:
What is little, what is great?
Howsoe'er the answer be,
Let me sing of what I know.

Comhairie Chonta
Átha Cliath Theas

ON A FORENOON OF SPRING

I'm glad I am alive, to see and feel
The full deliciousness of this bright day,
That's like a heart with nothing to conceal;
The young leaves scarcely trembling; the blue–grey
Rimming the cloudless ether far away;
Brairds, hedges, shadows; mountains that reveal
Soft sapphire; this great floor of polished steel
Spread out amidst the landmarks of the bay.
I stoop in sunshine to our circling net
From the black gunwale; tend these milky kine
Up their rough path; sit by yon cottage–door
Plying the diligent thread; take wings and soar–
O hark how with the season's laureate
Joy culminates in song! If such a song were mine!

MEADOWSWEET

Through grass, through amber'd cornfields, our slow Stream–
Fringed with its flags and reeds and rushes tall,
And Meadowsweet, the chosen of them all
By wandering children, yellow as the cream
Of those great cows–winds on as in a dream
By mill and footbridge, hamlet old and small
(Red roofs, gray tower), and sees the sunset gleam
On mullion'd windows of an ivied Hall.
There, once upon a time, the heavy King
Trod out its perfume from the Meadowsweet,
Strown like a woman's love beneath his feet,
In stately dance or jovial banqueting,
When all was new; and in its wayfaring
Our Streamlet curved, as now, through grass and wheat.

WRITING

A MAN who keeps a diary, pays
Due toll to many tedious days;
But life becomes eventful–then
His busy hand forgets the pen.
Most books, indeed, are records less
Of fulness than of emptiness.

ROBIN REDBREAST

Good–bye, good–bye to Summer,
For Summer's nearly done;
The garden smiling faintly,
Cool breezes in the sun;
Our Thrushes now are silent,
Our Swallows flown away–
But Robin's here, in coat of brown,
With ruddy breast–knot gay.
Robin, Robin Redbreast,
O Robin dear!
Robin singing sweetly
In the falling of the year.

Bright yellow, red, and orange,
The leaves come down in hosts;
The trees are Indian Princes,
But soon they'll turn to Ghosts;
The scanty pears and apples
Hang russet on the bough,
It's Autumn, Autumn, Autumn late,
'Twill soon be Winter now.
Robin, Robin, Redbreast,
O Robin dear!
And welaway! my Robin,
For pinching times are near.

The fireside for the Cricket,
The wheatstack for the Mouse,
When trembling night–winds whistle
And moan all round the house;
The frosty ways like iron,
The branches plumed with snow–
Alas! in Winter, dead and dark,
Where can poor Robin go?
Robin, Robin Redbreast,
O Robin dear!
And 'a crumb of bread for Robin,
His little heart to cheer.

DOWN ON THE SHORE

Down on the shore, on the sunny shore!
Where the salt smell cheers the land;
Where the tide moves bright under boundless light,
And the surge on the glittering strand;
Where the children wade in the shallow pools,
Or run from the froth in play;
Where the swift little boats with milk–white wings
Are crossing the sapphire bay,
And the ship in full sail, with a fortunate gale,
Holds proudy on her way;
Where the nets are spread on the grass to dry,
And asleep, hard by, the fishermen lie,
Under the tent of the warm blue sky,
With the hushing wave on its golden floor
To sing their lullaby.

Down on the shore, on the stormy shore!
Beset by a growling sea,
Whose mad waves leap on the rocky steep
Like wolves up a traveller's tree;
Where the foam flies wide, and an angry blast
Blows the curlew off, with a screech;
Where the brown sea–wrack, torn up by the roots,
Is flung out of fishes' reach;
And the tall ship rolls on the hidden shoals,
And scatters her planks on the beach;
Where slate and straw through the village spin,
And a cottage fronts the fiercest din
With a sailor's wife sitting sad within,
Hearkening the wind and the water's roar,
Till at last her tears begin.

A SEED

See how a Seed, which Autumn flung down,
And through the Winter neglected lay,
Uncoils two little green leaves and two brown,
With tiny root taking hold on the clay
As, lifting and strengthening day by day,
It pushes red branchless, sprouts new leaves,
And cell after cell the Power in it weaves
Out of the storehouse of soil and clime,
To fashion a Tree in due course of time;
Tree with rough bark and boughs' expansion,
Where the Crow can build his mansion,
Or a Man, in some new May,
Lie under whispering leaves and say,
"Are the ills of one's life so very bad
When a Green Tree makes me deliciously glad?"
As I do now. But where shall I be
When this little Seed is a tall green Tree?

LATE AUTUMN

October – and the skies are cool and gray
O'er stubbles emptied of their latest sheaf,
Bare meadow, and the slowly falling leaf.
The dignity of woods in rich decay
Accords full well with this majestic grief
That clothes our solemn purple hills to–day,
Whose afternoon is hush'd, and wintry brief
Only a robin sings from any spray.

And night sends up her pale cold moon, and spills
White mist around the hollows of the hills,
Phantoms of firth or lake; the peasant sees
His cot and stockyard, with the homestead trees,
Islanded; but no foolish terror thrills
His perfect harvesting; he sleeps at ease.

WAYSIDE FLOWERS

Pluck not the wayside flower,
It is the traveller's dower;
A thousand passers–by
Its beauties may espy,
May win a touch of blessing
From Nature's mild caressing.
The sad of heart perceives
A violet under leaves
Like sonic fresh–budding hope;
The primrose on the slope
A spot of sunshine dwells,
And cheerful message tells
Of kind renewing power;
The nodding bluebell's dye
Is drawn from happy sky.
Then spare the wayside flower!
It is the traveller's dower.

THESE LITTLE SONGS

These little Songs,
Found here and there,
Floating in air
By forest and lea,
Or hill–side heather,
In houses and throngs,
Or down by the sea –
Have come together,
How, I can't tell:
But I know full well
No witty goose–wing
On an inkstand begot 'em;
Remember each place
And moment of grace,
In summer or spring,
Winter or autumn
By sun, moon, stars,
Or a coal in the bars,
In market or church,
Graveyard or dance,
When they came without search,
Were found as by chance.
A word, a line,
You may say are mine;
But the best in the songs,
Whatever it be,
To you, and to me,
And to no one belongs.

THE DIRTY OLD MAN

A lay of Leadenhall

In a dirty old house lived a Dirty Old man;
Soap, towels, or brushes were not in his plan.
For forty long years, as the neighbours declared,
His house never once had been clean'd or repair'd.

"Twas a scandal and shame to the business–like street,
One terrible blot in a ledger so neat:
The shop full of hardware, but black as a hearse,
And the rest of the mansion a thousand times worse.

Outside, the old plaster, all spatter and stain,
Looked spotty in sunshine and streaky in rain;
The window–sills sprouted with mildewy grass,
And the panes from being broken were known to be glass.

On a ricketty signboard no learning could spell
The merchant who sol, or the goods he's to sell;
But for house and for man a new title took growth,
Like a fungus, – the Dirt gave a name to them both.

Within, there were carpets and cushions of dust,
The wood was half rot, and the metal half rust,
Old curtains half cobwebs, hung grimly aloof;
'Twas a Spiders' Elysium from cellar to roof.

There, king of the spiders, the Dirty Old Man
Lives busy and dirty as ever he can;
With dirt on his fingers and dirt on his face,
For the Dirty Old Man thinks the dirt no disgrace.

From his wig to his shoes, from his coat to his shirt,
His clothes are a proverb, a marvel of dirt;
The dirt is pervading, unfading, exceeding, –
Yet the Dirty Old Man has both learning and breeding.

Fine dames from their carriages, noble and fair,
Have enter'd his shop – less to buy than to stare;
And have afterwards said, though the dirt was so frightful,
The Dirty Man's manners were truly delightful.

Upstairs they don't venture, in dirt and in gloom, –
Mayn't peep at the door of the wonderful room
Such stories are told of, not half of them true;
The keyhole itself has no mortal seen through.

That room – forty years since, folk settled and deck'd it.
The luncheon's prepared, and the guests are expected.
The handsome young host he is gallant and gay,
For his love and her friends will be with him to–day.

With solid and dainty the table is drest,
The wine beams its brightest, the flowers bloom their best;
Yet the host need not smile, and no guests will appear,
For his sweetheart is dead, as he shortly shall hear.

Full forty years since, turn's the key in that door.
'Tis a room deaf and dumb 'mid the city's uproar.
The guests, for whose joyance that table was spread,
May now enter as ghosts, for they're every one dead.

Through a chink in the shutter dim lights come and go;
The seats are in order, the dishes a–row;
But the banquet was wealth to the rat and the mouse
Whose descendants have long left the Dirty Old House.

Cup and platter are mask'd in thick layers of dust;
The flowers fall'n to powder, the wine swath'd in crust;
A nosegay was laid before one special chair,
And the faded blue ribbon that bound it lies there.

The old man has play'd out his parts in the scene
Wherever he now is, I hope he's more clean.
Yet give we a thought free of scoffing or ban
To that Dirty Old House and that Dirty Old Man.,

AMY MARGARET

Amy Margaret's five years old,
Amy Margaret's hair is gold,
Dearer twenty–thousand–fold
Than gold, is Amy Margaret.

"Amy" is friend, is "Margaret"
The pearl for crown or carkanet?
Or peeping daisy, Summer's pet ?
Which are you, Amy Margaret?

A friend, a daisy, and a pearl;
A kindly, simple, precious– girl,
Such, howsoe'er the world may twirl,
Be ever,—Amy Margaret!

"Maids of Elsin-Mere"

2
Personal Selections of W.B. Yeats

KATE O' BELASHANNY

Seek up and down, both fair and brown,
We've purty lasses many, O;
But brown or fair, one girl most rare,
The Flow'r o' Belashanny, O.
As straight is she as poplar–tree
(Tho' not as aisy shaken, O,)
And walks so proud among the crowd,
For queen she might be taken, O.
From top to toe, where'er you go,
The loveliest girl of any, O,—
Ochone ! your mind I find unkind,
Sweet Kate o' Belashanny, O !

One summer day the banks were gay,
The Erne in sunshine glancin' there,
The big cascade its music play'd
And set the salmon dancin' there.
Along the green my Joy was seen;
Some goddess bright I thought her there;
The fishes, too, swam close, to view
Her image in the water there.
From top to toe, where'er you go,
The loveliest girl of any, O,—
Ochone! your mind I find unkind,
Sweet Kate o' Belashanny, O !

My dear, give ear!—the river's near,
And if you think I'm shammin' now,
To end my grief I'll seek relief
Among the trout and salmon, now;
For shrimps and sharks to make their marks,
And other watery vermin there;

Unless a mermaid saves my life,—
My wife, and me her merman there.
From top to toe, where'er you go,
The loveliest girl of any, O,—
Mavrone! your mind I find unkind,
Sweet Kate o' Belashanny, O !

'Tis all in vain that I complain;
No use to coax or chide her there;
As far away from me as Spain,
Although I stand beside her there.
O cruel Kate ! since that's my fate,
I'll look for love no more in you;
The seagull's screech as soon would reach
Your heart, as me implorin' you.
Tho' fair you are, and rare you are,
The loveliest flow'r of any, O,—
Too proud and high,—good–bye, say I,
To Kate o' Belashanny, O !

FOUR DUCKS ON A POND

Four ducks on a pond,
A grass–bank beyond,
A blue sky of spring,
White clouds on the wing;
What a little thing
To remember for years—
To remember with tears!

THE LOVER AND BIRDS

Within a budding grove,
In April's ear sang every bird his best,
But not a song to pleasure my unrest,
Or touch the tears unwept of bitter love;
Some spake, methought, with pity, some as if in jest.
To every word
Of every bird
I listen'd, and replied as it behove.

Scream'd Chaffinch, 'Sweet, sweet, sweet!
Pretty lovey, come and meet me here !'
'Chaffinch,' quoth I, 'be dumb awhile, in fear
Thy darling prove no better than a cheat,
And never come, or fly when wintry days appear.'
Yet from a twig,
With voice so big,
The little fowl his utterance did repeat.

Then I, 'The man forlorn
Hears Earth send up a foolish noise aloft.'
'And what'll he do ? What'll he do ?' scoff'd
The Blackbird, standing, in an ancient thorn,
Then spread his sooty wings and flitted to the croft
With cackling laugh;
Whom I, being half
Enraged, called after, giving back his scorn.

Worse mock'd the Thrush, 'Die ! die !
Oh, could he do it ? could he do it ? Nay !

Be quick ! be quick ! Here, here, here !' (went his lay.)
'Take heed ! take heed ! 'then 'Why ? why ? why ? why ? why ?
See–ee now ! see–ee now !' (he drawl'd) 'Back ! back !
back ! R–r–r–run away !'
O Thrush, be still !
Or at thy will,
Seek some less sad interpreter than I.

'Air, air ! blue air and white !
Whither I flee, whither, O whither, O whither I flee!'
(Thus the Lark hurried, mounting from the lea)
'Hills, countries, many waters glittering bright,
Whither I see, whither I see ! deeper, deeper, deeper,
whither I see, see, see !'

'Gay Lark,' I said,
"The song that's bred
In happy nest may well to heaven make flight."

"There's something, something sad,
I half remember"—piped a broken strain.
Well sung, sweet Robin ! Robin sung again.
"Spring's opening cheerily, cheerily ! be we glad !"
Which moved, I wist not why, me melancholy mad,
Till now, grown meek,
With wetted cheek,
Most comforting and gentle thoughts I had.

TWILIGHT VOICES

Now, at the hour when ignorant mortals
Drowse in the shade of their whirling sphere,
Heaven and Hell from invisible portals
Breathing comfort and ghastly fear,
Voices I hear;
I hear strange voices, flitting, calling,
Wavering by on the dusky blast,—
"Come, let us go, for the night is falling;
Come, let us go, for the day is past !"

Troops of joys are they, now departed?
Winged hopes that no longer stay?
Guardian spirits grown weary–hearted?
Powers that have linger'd their latest day?
What do they say ?
What do they sing ? I hear them calling,
Whispering, gathering, flying fast,—
"Come, come, for the night is falling;
Come, come, for the day is past !"

Sing they to me —"Thy taper's wasted;
Mortal, thy sands of life run low;
Thine hours like a flock of birds have hasted:
Time is ending;—we go, we go."
Sing they so ?
Mystical voices, floating, calling;
Dim farewells—the last, the last ?
Come, come away, the night is falling;
"Come, come away, the day is past."

See, I am ready, Twilight voices !
Child of the spirit–world am I;
How should I fear you ? my soul rejoices,
O speak plainer ! O draw nigh !
Fain would I fly !
Tell me your message, Ye who are calling
Out of the dimness vague and vast;
Lift me, take me,—the night is falling;
Quick, let us go,—the day is past.

AEOLIAN HARP

What is it that is gone, we fancied ours ?
Oh what is lost that never may be told?—
We stray all afternoon, and we may grieve
Until the perfect closing of the night.
Listen to us, thou gray Autumnal Eve,
Whose part is silence. At thy verge the clouds
Are broken into melancholy gold;
The waifs of Autumn and the feeble flow'rs
Glimmer along our woodlands in wet light;
Within thy shadow thou dost weave the shrouds
Of joy and great adventure, waxing cold,
Which once, or so it seemed, were full of might.
Some power it was, that lives not with us now,
A thought we had, but could not, could not hold.
O sweetly, swiftly pass'd:—air sings and murmurs;
Green leaves are gathering on the dewy bough;
O sadly, swiftly pass'd:—air sighs and mutters;
Red leaves are dropping on the rainy mould.
Then comes the snow, unfeatured, vast, and white.
O what is gone from us, we fancied ours?—

THE NOBLEMAN'S WEDDING

I once was a guest at a Nobleman's wedding;
Fair was the Bride, but she scarce had been kind,
And now in our mirth, she had tears nigh the shedding
Her former true lover still runs in her mind.

Attired like a minstrel, her former true lover
Takes up his harp, and runs over the strings;
And there among strangers, his grief to discover,
A fair maiden's falsehood he bitterly sings.

"Now here is the token of gold that was broken;
Seven long years it was kept for your sake;
You gave it to me as a true lover's token;
No longer I'll wear it, asleep or awake."

She sat in her place by the head of the table,
The words of his ditty she mark'd them right well:
To sit any longer this bride was not able,
So down at the bridegroom's feet she fell.

"O one, one request, my lord, one and no other,
O this one request will you grant it to me?
To lie for this night in the arms of my mother,
And ever, and ever thereafter with thee."

Her one, one request it was granted her fairly;
Pale were her cheeks as she went up to bed;
And the very next morning, early, early,
They rose and they found this young bride was dead.

The bridegroom ran quickly, he held her, he kiss'd her,
He spoke loud and low, and listen'd full fain;
He call'd on her waiting–maids round to assist her
But nothing could bring the lost breath back again.

O carry her softly! the grave is made ready;
At head and at foot plant a laurel–bush green;
For she was a young and a sweet noble lady,
The fairest young bride that I ever have seen.

THE GIRL'S LAMENTATION

With grief and mourning I sit to spin;
My Love passed by, and he didn't come in;
He passes by me, both day and night,
And carries off my poor heart's delight.

There is a tavern in yonder town,
My Love goes there and he spends a crown;
He takes a strange girl upon his knee,
And never more gives a thought to me.

Says he, "We'll wed without loss of time,
And sure our love's but a little crime;"—
My apron–string now it's wearing short,
And my Love he seeks other girls to court.

O with him I'd go if I had my will,
I'd follow him barefoot o'er rock and hill;
I'd never once speak of all my grief
If he'd give me a smile for my heart's relief.

In our wee garden the rose unfolds,
With bachelor's–buttons and marigolds;
I'll tie no posies for dance or fair,
A willow–twig is for me to wear.

For a maid again I can never be,
Till the red rose blooms on the willow tree.
Of such a trouble I've heard them tell,
And now I know what it means full well.

As through the long lonesome night I lie,
I'd give the world if I might but cry;
But I mus' n't moan there or raise my voice,
And the tears run down without any noise.

And what, O what will my mother say?
She'll wish her daughter was in the clay.
My father will curse me to my face;
The neighbours will know of my black disgrace.

My sister's buried three years, come Lent;
But sure we made far too much lament.
Beside her grave they still say a prayer—
I wish to God 'twas myself was there !

The Candlemas crosses hang near my bed;
To look at them puts me much in dread,
They mark the good time that's gone and past:
It's like this year's one will prove the last.

The oldest cross it's a dusty brown,
But the winter winds didn't shake it down;
The newest cross keeps the colour bright;
When the straw was reaping my heart was light.

The reapers rose with the blink of morn,
And gaily stook'd up the yellow corn;
To call them home to the field I'd run,
Through the blowing breeze and the summer sun.

When the straw was weaving my heart was glad,
For neither sin nor shame I had,
In the barn where oat–chaff was flying round,
And the thumping flails made a pleasant sound.

Now summer or winter to me it's one;
But oh ! for a day like the time that's gone.
I'd little care was it storm or shine,
If I had but peace in this heart of mine.

Oh ! light and false is a young man's kiss,
And a foolish girl gives her soul for this.
Oh ! light and short is the young man's blame,
And a helpless girl has the grief and shame.

To the river–bank once I thought to go,
And cast myself in the stream below;
I thought 'twould carry us far out to sea,
Where they'd never find my poor babe and me.

Sweet Lord, forgive me that wicked mind!
You know I used to be well–inclined.
Oh, take compassion upon my state,
Because my trouble is so very great.

My head turns round with the spinning wheel,
And a heavy cloud on my eyes I feel.
But the worst of all is at my heart's core;
For my innocent days will come back no more.

THE RUINED CHAPEL

By the shore, a plot of ground
Clips a ruin'd chapel round,
Buttress'd with a grassy mound;
Where Day and Night and Day go by,
And bring no touch of human sound.

Washing of the lonely seas,
Shaking of the guardian trees,
Piping of the salted breeze;
Day and Night and Day go by
To the endless tune of these.

Or when, as winds and waters keep
A hush more dead than any sleep,
Still morns to stiller evenings creep,
And Day and Night and Day go by;
Here the silence is most deep.

The empty ruins, lapsed again
Into Nature's wide domain,
Sow themselves with seed and grain
As Day and Night and Day go by;
And hoard June's sun and April's rain.

Here fresh funeral tears were shed;
Now the graves are also dead;
And suckers from the ash–tree spread,
While Day and Night and Day go by;–
And stars move calmly overhead.

THE LEPRACAUN OR FAIRY SHOEMAKER

Little Cowboy, what have you heard,
Up on the lonely rath's green mound?
Only the plaintive yellow bird
Sighing in sultry fields around,
Chary, chary, chary, chee–ee!—
Only the grasshopper and the bee?—
"Tip–tap, rip–rap,
Tick–a–tack–too !
Scarlet leather, sewn together,
This will make a shoe.
Left, right, pull it tight;
Summer days are warm;
Underground in winter,
Laughing at the storm!"
Lay your ear close to the hill.
Do you not catch the tiny clamour,
Busy click of an elfin hammer,
Voice of the Lepracaun singing shrill
As he merrily plies his trade
He's a span
And a quarter in height.
Get him in sight, hold him tight,
And you're a made
Man !

You watch your cattle the summer day,
Sup on potatoes, sleep in the hay;
How would you like to roll in your carriage,
Look for a duchess's daughter in marriage?
Seize the Shoemaker—then you may!
"Big boots a–hunting,
Sandals in the hall,
White for a wedding–feast,
Pink for a ball.
This way, that way,
So we make a shoe;
Getting rich every stitch,
Tick–tack–too!"
Nine–and–ninety treasure–crocks

This keen miser–fairy hath,
Hid in mountains, woods, and rocks,
Ruin and round–tow'r, cave and rath,
And where the cormorants build;
From times of old
Guarded by him;
Each of them fill'd
Full to the brim
With gold !

I caught him at work one day, myself,
In the castle–ditch where foxglove grows,—
A wrinkled, wizen'd, and bearded Elf,
Spectacles stuck on his pointed nose,
Silver buckles to his hose,
Leather apron—shoe in his lap—
"Rip–rap, tip–tap,
Tick–tack–too!
(A grasshopper on my cap!
Away the moth flew!)
Buskins for a fairy prince,
Brogues for his son,—
Pay me well, pay me well,
When the job is done !"
The rogue was mine, beyond a doubt.
I stared at him; he stared at me;
"Servant, Sir !" "Humph!" says he,
And pull'd a snuff–box out.
He took a long pinch, look'd better pleased,
The queer little Lepracaun;
Offer'd the box with a whimsical grace,—
Pouf! he flung the dust in my face,
And while I sneezed,
Was gone!

THE MAIDS OF ELSIN–MERE

When the spinning–room was here
Came Three Damsels, clothed in white,
With their spindles every night;
One and Two and three fair Maidens,
Spinning to a pulsing cadence,
Singing songs of Elsin–Mere;
Till the eleventh hour was toll'd,
Then departed through the wold.
Years ago, and years ago;
And the tall reeds sigh as the wind doth blow.

Three white Lilies, calm and clear,
And they were loved by every one;
Most of all, the Pastor's Son,
Listening to their gentle singing,
Felt his heart go from him, clinging
Round these Maids of Elsin–Mere.
Sued each night to make them stay,
Sadden'd when they went away.
Years ago, and years ago;
And the tall reeds sigh as the wind doth blow.

Hands that shook with love and fear
Dared put back the village clock,—
Flew the spindle, turn'd the rock,
Flow'd the song with subtle rounding,
Till the false 'eleven' was sounding;
Then these Maids of Elsin–Mere
Swiftly, softly, left the room,
Like three doves on snowy plume.
Years ago, and years ago;
And the tall reeds sigh as the wind doth blow

One that night who wander'd near
Heard lamentings by the shore,
Saw at dawn three stains of gore
In the waters fade and dwindle.
Never more with song and spindle
Saw we Maids of Elsin–Mere,

The Pastor's Son did pine and die;
Because true love should never lie.
Years ago, and years ago;
And the tall reeds sigh as the wind doth blow.

A DREAM

I heard the dogs howl in the moonlight night;
I went to the window to see the sight;
All the Dead that ever I knew
Going one by one and two by two.

On they pass'd, and on they pass'd;
Townsfellows all, from first to last;
Born in the moonlight of the lane,
Quench'd in the heavy shadow again.

Schoolmates, marching as when we play'd
At soldiers once—but now more staid;
Those were the strangest sight to me
Who were drown'd, I knew, in the awful sea.
Straight and handsome folk; bent and weak, too;
Some that I loved, and gasp'd to speak to;
Some but a day in their churchyard bed;
Some that I had not known were dead.

A long, long crowd—where each seem'd lonely,
Yet of them all there was one, one only,
Raised a head or look'd my way:
She linger'd a moment—she might not stay.

How long since I saw that fair pale face!
Ah! Mother dear ! might I only place
My head on thy breast, a moment to rest,
While thy hand on my tearful cheek were prest!

On, on, a moving bridge they made
Across the moon–stream, from shade to shade,
Young and old, women and men;
Many long–forgot, but remember'd then.

And first there came a bitter laughter;
A sound of tears the moment after;
And then a music so lofty and gay,
That every morning, day by day,
I strive to recall it if I may.

St. Anne's Church, Ballyshannon.

THE ABBOT OF INNISFALLEN

The Abbot of Innisfallen
awoke ere dawn of day;
Under the dewy green leaves
went he forth to pray.

The lake around his island
lay smooth and dark and deep,
And wrapt in a misty stillness
the mountains were all asleep.

Low kneel'd the Abbot Cormac
when the dawn was dim and gray;
The prayers of his holy office
he faithfully 'gan say.

Low kneel'd the Abbot Cormac
while the dawn was waxing red;
And for his sins' forgiveness
a solemn prayer he said:

Low kneel'd that holy Abbot
while the dawn was waxing clear;
And he pray'd with loving–kindness
for his convent–brethren dear.

Low kneel'd that blessed Abbot
while the dawn was waxing bright;
He pray'd a great prayer for Ireland,
he pray'd with all his might.

Low kneel'd that good old Father
while the sun began to dart;
He pray'd a prayer for all men,
he pray'd it from his heart.

His blissful soul was in Heaven,
tho' a breathing man was he;
He was out of time's dominion,
so far as the living may be.

The Abbot of Innisfallen
arose upon his feet;
He heard a small bird singing,
and O but it sung sweet!

It sung upon a holly–bush,
this little snow–white bird;
A song so full of gladness
he never before had heard.

It sung upon a hazel,
it sung upon a thorn;
He had never heard such music
since the hour that he was born.

It sung upon a sycamore,
it sung upon a briar;
To follow the song and hearken
this Abbot could never tire.

Till at last he well bethought him;
he might no longer stay;
So he bless'd the little white singing–bird,
and gladly went his way.

But, when he came to his Abbey,
he found a wondrous change;
He saw no friendly faces there,
for every face was strange.

The strange men spoke unto him;
and he heard from all and each
The foreign tongue of the Sassenach,
not wholesome Irish speech.

Then the oldest monk came forward,
in Irish tongue spake he:
"Thou wearest the holy Augustine's dress,
and who hath given it to thee?"

"I wear the Augustine's dress,
and Cormac is my name,
The Abbot of this good abbey
by grace of God I am.

Went forth to pray, at the dawn of day;
and when my prayers were said,
I hearken'd awhile to a little bird,
that sung above my head."

The monks to him made answer,
Two hundred years have gone o'er,
Since our Abbot Cormac went through the gate,
and never was heard of more.

Matthias now is our Abbot,
and twenty have pass'd away.
The stranger is lord of Ireland;
we live in an evil day."

"Days will come and go," he said,
"and the world will pass away,
In Heaven a day is a thousand years,
a thousand years are a day."

"Now give me absolution;
for my time is come," said he.
And they gave him absolution,
as speedily as might be.

Then, close outside the window,
the sweetest song they heard
That ever yet since the world began
was utter'd by any bird.

The monks look'd out and saw the bird,
its feathers all white and clean;
And there in a moment, beside it,
another white bird was seen.

Those two they sang together,
waved their white wings, and fled;
Flew aloft, and vanish'd;
but the good old man was dead.

They buried his blessed body
where lake and green-sward meet;
A carven cross above his head,
a holly-bush at his feet;

Where spreads the beautiful water
to gay or cloudy skies,
And the purple peaks of Killarney
from ancient woods arise.

ABBEY ASAROE

Gray, gray is Abbey Asaroe,
by Belashanny town,
It has neither door nor window,
the walls are broken down;
The carven–stones lie scatter'd
in briar and nettle–bed;
The only feet are those that come
at burial of the dead.
A little rocky rivulet
runs murmuring to the tide,
Singing a song of ancient days,
in sorrow, not in pride;
The boortree and the lightsome ash
across the portal grow,
And heaven itself is now the roof
of Abbey Asaroe.

It looks beyond the harbour–stream
to Gulban mountain blue;
It hears the voice of Erna's fall,—
Atlantic breakers too;
High ships go sailing past it;
the sturdy clank of oars
Brings in the salmon–boat to haul
a net upon the shores;
And this way to his home–creek,
when the summer day is done,
Slow sculls the weary fisherman
across the setting sun;
While green with corn is Sheegus Hill,
his cottage white below;
But gray at every season
is Abbey Asaroe.

There stood one day a poor old man
above its broken bridge;
He heard no running rivulet,
he saw no mountain–ridge;
He turn'd his back on Sheegus Hill,
and view'd with misty sight
The Abbey walls, the burial–ground
with crosses ghostly white;
Under a weary weight of years
he bow'd upon his staff,
Perusing in the present time
the former's epitaph;
For, gray and wasted like the walls,
a figure full of woe,
This man was of the blood of them
who founded Asaroe.

From Derry to Bundrowas Tower,
Tirconnell broad was theirs;
Spearmen and plunder, bards and wine,
and holy abbot's prayers;
With chanting always in the house
which they had builded high
To God and to Saint Bernard,—
where at last they came to die.
At worst, no workhouse grave for him !
the ruins of his race
Shall rest among the ruin'd stones
of this their saintly place.

The fond old man was weeping;
and tremulous and slow
Along the rough and crooked lane
he crept from Asaroe.

"Vignette and Ornaments"

3
The Music Master

A LOVE STORY – THE MUSIC–MASTER – Part 1

I

Music and Love! – If lovers hear me sing,
I will for them essay the simple take,
To hold some fair young listeners in a ring
With echoes gather'd from an Irish vale,
Where still, methinks, abide my golden years,
Though I not with them, – far discern'd through tears.

II

When evening fell upon the village street
And brother fields, reposing hand in hand,
Unlike where flaring cities scorn to meet
The kiss of dusk that quiets all the land,
'Twas pleasant laziness to loiter by
Houses and cottages, a friendly spy.

III

And hear the frequent fiddle that would glide
Through jovial mazes of a jig or reel,
Or sink from sob to sob with plaintive slide,
Or mount the steps of swift exulting zeal;
For our old village was with music fill'd
Like any grove where thrushes wont to build.

IV

Mixt with the roar of bellows and of flame,
Perhaps the reed–voice of a clarionet
From forge's open ruddy shutter came;
Or round some hearth were silent people set,
Where the low flute, with plaintive quivering, ran on
Through "Coleen Dheas" or "Hawk or Ballyshannon."

V

Or pictured on those bygone, shadowy nights
I see a group of girls at needlework,
Placed round a candle throwing soft half–lights
On the contrasted face, and the dark
And fair–hair'd head, a bunch of human flow'rs;
And many a ditty cheers th' industrious hours.

VI

Pianoforte' sound from curtain's pane
Would join the lofty to the lowly roof
In the sweet links of one harmonious chain;
And often down the street some Glee's old woof,
"Hope of my heart" – "Ye Shepherds" – "Lightly tread,"
Would mesh my steps or wrap me in my bed.

VII

The most delicious chance, if we should hear,
Pour'd from our climbing glen's enfoliaged rocks,
At dusk some solitary bugle, clear,
Remote, and melancholy; echo mocks
The strain delighted, wafting it afar
Up to the threshold of the evening star.

III

And Gerald was our music–master's name;
Young Gerald White; whose mother, not long wed,
Only to make him ours by birthright came.
Her Requiescat I have often read,
Where thickest ivy hangs its ancient pall
Over the dumb and desolate abbey wall.

IX

The father found a music–pupil rare,
More ready still to learn than he to teach;
His art no longer was his only care,
But now young Gerald with it, each for each;
And with a secret and assiduous joy
The grave musician taught his happy boy.

X

The boy's whole thought to Music lean'd and sway'd;
He heard a minor in the wind at night,
And many a tune the village noises play'd;
The thunder roar'd like bands before the might
Of marching armies; in deep summer calm
The falling brooklet would intone a psalm.

XI

The Chapel organ–loft, his father's seat,
Was to the child his earthly paradise;
And that celestial one that used to greet
His infant dreams, could take no other guise
Than visions of green curtains and gold pipes,
And angles of whom quire–girls were the types.

XII

Their fresh young voices from the congregation,
Train'd and combined by simple rules of chant,
And lifted on the harmonious modulation
Roll'd from the lofty organ, ministrant
To sacred triumph, well might bring a thought
Of angels there, – perhaps themselves it brought.

XIII

Poor girls the most were: this one had her nest,
A mountain mavis, in the craggy furze
Another in close lane must toil and rest,
And never cage–bird's song more fine than hers,
Humming at work all through the busy week,
Set free in Sabbath chorus, proud and meek.

XIV

And when young Gerald might adventure forth
Through Music–land, – where hope and memory kiss
And singing fly beyond the bourne of earth,
And the whole spirit full of aching bliss
Would follow as the parting shrouds reveal
Glimpses ineffable, but soon conceal, –

XV

While all the hills, mayhap, and distant plain,
Village and brook were shaded, fold on fold,
With the slow dusk, and on the purpling pane
Soft twilight barr'd with crimson and with gold
Lent to that simple little house of prayer
A richly solemn, a cathedral air;

XVI

His symphonies to suit the dying close
Suffused it with a voice that could not ask
In vain for tears; not ask in vain from those
Who in the dew fulfill'd their pious task,
Kneeling with rosaries beside a grave;
To whom a heavenly comforting it gave.

XVII

Thus village years went by. Day after day
Flow'd, as a stream unvext with storms or floods
Flows by some islet with a hawthorn grey;
Where circling seasons bring a share of buds,]
Nests, blossoms, ruddy fruit, and, in their turn,
Of withering leaves and frosty twigs forlorn.

XVIII

So went the years, that never may abide;
Boyhood to manhood, manly prime to age,
Ceaselessly gliding on, as still they glide; –
Until the father yields for heritage
(Joyful, yet with a sigh) the master's place
To Gerald – who could higher fortune grace.

XIX

But the shy youth has yet his hours of leisure:
And now, the Spring upon the emerald hills
Dancing with flying clouds, how keen his pleasure,
Plunged in deep glens or tracking upland rills,
Till lessening light recall him from his roaming
To breathe his gather'd secrets to the gloaming.

XX

Spring was around him, and within him too.
Delightful season! – life without a spur
Bounds gaily forward, and the heart is new
As the green want fresh budded on a fir;
And Nature, into jocund chorus waking,
Tempts every young voice to her merry–making.

XXI

Gerald, high echoing this delightful Spring,
Pour'd from his finger–tips electric power
In audible creations swift of wing,
Till sunshine glimpsing through an April shower,
And clouds, and delicate glories, and the bound
Of lucid sky came melting into sound.

XXII

Our ear receives in common with our eye
One Beauty, flowing through a different gate,
With melody its form, and harmony
Its hue; one mystic Beauty is the mate
Of Spirit indivisible, one love
Her look, her voice, her memory do move.

XXIII

Yet sometimes in his playing came a tone
Not learn'd of sun or shadow, wind or brook,
But thoughts so much his own he dared not own,
Nor, prizing much, appraise them; dared not look
In fear to lose an image undefined
That brighten'd every vista of his mind.

XXIV

Two pupils dwelt upon the river–side,
At Cloonamore, a cottage near the rush
Of narrow'd waters breaking from a wide
And pond–like smoothness, brimming green and flush
Dark groves; and here for Gerald, truth to say,
His weekly task was more than holiday.

XXV

A quiet home it was; compact and neat
As a wren's nest. A gentle woman's choice
Had built and beautified the green retreat;
But in her labours might she not rejoice,
Being summon'd to a stiller place of rest;
And spent her last breath in a dear behest.

XXVI

That was for her two daughters: she had wed
A plain, rough husband, though a kind and true;
And "Dearest Bernard," from her dying bed
She whisper'd. "Promise me you'll try to do
For Ann and Milly what was at my heart,
If God had spared me to perform my part."

XXVII

As well as no abundant purse allow'd.
Or as the neighbouring village could supply,
The father kept his promise, and was proud
To see the girls grow up beneath his eye
Two ladies in their culture and their mien;
Though not the less there lay a gulf between.

XXVIII

A spirit unrefined the elder had,
An envious eye, a tongue of petty scorn.
That women these may own – how true! how sad!
And these, though Ann had been a countess born,
Had mark'd her meaner to the dullest sight
Than stands a yellow lily with a white.

XXIX

White lily, – Milly, – darling little girl!
I think I see as once I saw her stand;
Her soft hair waving in a single curl
Behind her ear; a kid licking her hand;
Her fair young face with health and racing warm.
And loose frock blown about her slender form.

XXX

The dizzy lark, a dot on the white cloud,
That sprinkles music o'er the vernal breeze,
Was not more gay than Milly's joyous mood;
The silent lark that starry twilight sees
Cradled among the braird in closest bower,
Not more quiescent than her tranquil hour.

XXXI

Her mind was open, as a flowery cup
That gathers richness from the sun and dew,
To knowledge, and as easily drew up
The wholesome sap of life; unwatch'd it grew,
A lovely blossom in a shady place;
And like her mind, so was her innocent face.

XXII

At all times fair, it never look'd so fair
As when the holy glow of harmonies
Lighted it through; her spirit as it were
An azure heav'n outshining at her eyes;
With Gerald's tenor while the fountain sprung
Of her contralto, fresh and pure and young.

XXXIII

In years a child when lessons thus began,
Child is she still, yet nearly woman grown;
For childhood stays with woman more than man,
In voice and cheek and mouth, nor these alone;
And up the sky with no intense revealing
May the great dawn of womanhood come stealing.

XXXIV

Now must the moon of childhood's trembling white
Faint in the promise of her flushing heaven;
Looks are turn'd eastward, where new orient light
Suffuses all the air with subtle leaven;
And shadowy mountain–paths begin to show
Their unsuspected windings 'mid the glow.

XXXV

Her silky locks have ripen'd into brown,
Her soft blue eyes grown deeper and more shy,
And lightly on her lifted head the crown
Of queenly maidenhood sits meek and high;
Her frank soul lies in her ingenuous voice,
Most purely tuned to sorrow or rejoice.

XXXVI

Within the Chapel on a Sunday morn
She bows her mild head near the altar–rail,
And raises up that mild full voice unworn
Into the singing; – should a Sunday fail,
There's one would often mark her empty seat,
There's one would find their anthem incomplete.

XXXVII

Few her companions are, and few her books;
And in a ruin'd convent's circling shade,
The loveliest of tranquil river–nooks.
Where trailing birch, fit bow'r for gentle maid,
And feather'd fir–tree half shut out the stream,
She often sits alone to read or dream.

XXXVIII

Sometimes through leafy lattice she espies
A flitting figure on the other shore;
But ever past th' enchanted precinct hies
That wanderer, and where the rapids roar
Through verdured crags, shelters his beating heart,
Foolishly bent to seek, yet stay apart.

XXXIX

Then Milly can resume her reverie,
About a real friend, that she could love;
But finds her broken thought is apt to flee
To what seem other musings: slowly move
The days, and counted days move ever slowest:
Milly! How long ere thy own heart thou knowest?

XL

Sooner than Gerald his. His path–side birds
Are scarcely more unconscious or more shrinking.
And pray too for your poor old nurse, asthore;
Your own true mother scarce could love you more!"

XLVI

Slow were their feet amongst the many graves,
Over the stile and up the chapel walk,
Where stood the poplars with their timid leaves
Hung motionless on every slender stalk.
The air in one hot calm appear'd to lie,
And thunder mutter'd in the heavy sky.

XLVII

Along the street was heard the laughing sound
Of boys at play, who knew no thought of death;
Deliberate–stepping cows, to milking bound,
Lifted their heads and low'd with fragrant breath;
The women knitting at their thresholds cast
A look upon our stranger as he pass'd

XLVIII

Their pathway foliage–curtain'd and moss–grown;–
Behind the trees the white flood flashing swift,
Through many moist and ferny rocks flung down,
Roars steadily, where sunlights play and shift.
How oft they stop, how long, they nothing know,
Nor how the pulses of the evening go.

XLIV

Their talk? – the dappled hyacinthine glade
Lit up in points of blue, – how soft the treble
The kine's deep lowing is by distance made, –
The quail's "twit–wit–wit," like a hopping pebble
Thrown along ice, – the dragonflies, the birds,
The rustling twig, – all noticed in few words.

XLV

A level pond, inlaid with lucid shadows
Of groves and crannied cliffs and evening sky,
And rural domes of hay, where the green meadows
Slope to embrace its margin peacefully.
The slumb'ring river to the rapid draws;
And here, upon a grassy jut, they pause,

XLVI

How shy a strength is Love's, that so much fears
Its darling secret to itself to won!
Their rapt, illimitable mood appears
A beauteous miracle for each alone;
Exalted high above all range of hope
By the pure soul's eternity of scope.

XLVII

Yet in both ears a prophecy is breathed
Of how this evening's phantom may arise,
In richer hues than ever sunlight wreathed
On hill or wood or wave: in brimming eyes
The glowing landscape melts away from each;
And full their bosoms swell, too full for speech.

XLVIII

Is it a dream? The countless happy stars
Stand silently into the deepening blue;
In slow procession all the molten bars
Of cloud move down; the air is dim with dew;
Eve scatters roses on the shroud of day;
The common world sinks far and far away.

XLIX

With goodnight kiss the zephyr, half asleep,
Sinks to its cradle in the dusk of trees,
Where river–chimings tolling sweet and deep
Make lullaby, and all field–scents that please
The Summer's children float into the gloom
Dream–interwoven in a viewless loom.

L

Clothed with an earnest paleness, not a blush,
And with th'angelic gravity of love,
Each lover's face amid the twilight hush
Is like a saint's whose thoughts are all above
In perfect gratitude for heavenly boon;
And o'er them for a halo comes the moon.

LI

Thus through the leaves and the dim dewy croft
They longer homeward. Flowers around their feet
Bless them, and in the firmament aloft
Night's silent ardours. And an hour too fleet,
Through stretching years from all the life before,
Conducts their footsteps to her cottage door.

LII

Thenceforth they meet more timidly? – in truth,
Some lovers might, but all are not the same;
In the clear ether of their simple youth
Steady and white ascends the sacred flame.
They do not shrink hereafter; rather seek
More converse, but with graver voices speak.

LIII

One theme at last preferred to every other,
Joying to talk of that mysterious land
Where each enshrines the image of a mother
Best of all watchers in the guardian band;
To highest, tenderest thought is freedom given
Amid this unembarrass'd air of Heaven.

LIV

For when a hymn has wing'd itself away
On Palestrina's full–resounding chords,
And at the trellis'd window loiter they,
Deferring their goodnight with happy words,
Almost they know, without a throb of fear,
Of spirits in the twilight standing near.

LV

And day by day and week by week pass by,
And Love still poised upon a trembling plume
Floats on the very verge of sovereignty,
Where ev'n a look may call him to assume
The rich apparel and the shining throne,
And claim two loyal subjects for his own.

LVI

Wondrous, that first, full, mutual look of love
Coming ere either looker is aware;
Unbounded trust, a tenderness above
All tenderness; mute music, speechless pray'r
Life's mystery, reality, and might,
Soft–swimming in a single ray of light!

LVII

O when shall fly this talismanic gleam,
Which melts like lightning every prison–bar,
Which penetrates the mist with keener beam
Than flows from sun or moon of any star?
Love waits; and like a pebble of the ground
Th' imperial gem lies willing to be found.

LVIII

One evening, Gerald came before his hour,
Distrustful of the oft–consulted clock;
And waits, with no companion, till his flow'r –
Keeping the time as one of Flora's flock,
Whose shepherdess, the Sunset Star, doth fold
Each in its leaves – he may again behold.

LIX

Nor thinks it long. Familiar all, and dear,
A sanctity pervades the silent room.
Autumnal is the season of the year;
A mystic softness and love–weighty gloom
Gather with twilight. In a dream he lays
His hand on the piano, dreaming plays.

LX

Most faint and broken sounds at first are stealing
Into the shadowy stillness; wild and slow,
Imperfect cadences of captive feeling,
Gathering its strength, and yet afraid to know
Its chance of freedom, – till on murmuring chords
Th' unguarded thought strays forth in passionate words.

LXI

Angel of Music! When our finest speech
Is all too coarse to give the heart relief,
The inmost fountains lie within thy reach,
Soother of every joy and every grief;
And to the stumbling word thou lendest winds
On which aloft th' enfranchised spirit springs.

LXII

Much love may in not many words be told;
And on the sudden love can speak the best.
These mystical melodious buds unfold,
On very petal showing clear imprest
The name of Love. So Gerald sung and play'd
Unconscious of himself, in twilight shade.

LXIII

He has not overheard (O might it be!)
This stifled sobbing at the open door,
Where Milly stands arrested tremblingly
By that which in an instant tells her more
Than all the dumb months mused of; tells it plain
To joy that cannot comprehend its gain.

LXIV

One moment, and they shall be face to face,
Free in the gift of this great confidence.
Wrapt in the throbbing calm of its embrace,
No more to disunite their spirits thence.
The myrtle crown stoops close to either brow, –
But ah! What alien voice distracts them now?

LXV

Her sister comes. And Milly turns away;
Hurriedly bearing to some quiet spot
Her tears and her full heart, longing to lay
On a dim pillow cheeks so moist and hot.
When midnight stars between her curtains gleam
Fair Milly sleeps, and dreams a happy dream.

LXVI

O dream, poor child! Beneath the midnight stars;
O slumber through the kindling of the dawn;
The shadow's on its way; the storm that mars
The lily even now is hurrying on.
All has been long fulfill'd; yet I could weep
At thought of thee so quietly asleep.

LXVII

But Gerald, through the night serenely spread,
Walks quickly home, intoxicate with bliss
Not named and not examined; overhead
The clustering lights of worlds are full of this
New element; the soft wind's dusky wings
Grow warmer on his cheek, with whisperings.

LXVIII

And yet to–night he has not seen his Love,
His Love – in that one word all comfort dwells;
Reaching from earth to those clear flames above,
And making common food of miracles.
Kind pulsing Nature, touch of Deity,
Sure thou art full of love, which lovers see!

LXIX

Most cruel Nature, so unmoved, so hard,
The while thy children shake with joy or pain!
Thou wilt not forward Love, nor Death retard
One finger–push, for mortal's dearest gain.
Our Gerald, through the night serenely spread,
Walks quickly home, and finds his father dead.

LXX

God's awe must be where the last stroke comes down,
Though but the ending of a weary strife,
Though years on years weigh low the hoary crown,
Or sickness tenant all the house of life;
Stupendous ever is the great event,
The frozen form most strangely different!

LXXI

To Gerald follow'd many doleful days,
Like wet clouds moving through a sullen sky.
A vast unlook'd–for change the mind dismays,
And smites its world with instability;
Books appear quaking, towers and treasures vain,
Peace foolish, Joy disgusting, Hope insane.

LXXII

For even Cloonamore, that image dear,
Returns to Gerald's mind like its own ghost,
In melancholy garments, drench'd and sere,
Its joy, its colour, and its welcome lost.
Wanting one token sure to lean upon.
(How almost gain'd!) his happy dream is gone.

LXXIII

Distracted purposes, a homeless band,
Throng in his meditation – now he flies
To rest his soul on Milly's cheek and hand, –
Now he makes outcry on his fantasies
For busy cheats: the lesson not yet learn'd
How Life's true coast from vapour is discern'd.

LXXIV

Ah me! 'tis like the tolling of a bell
To hear it – " Past is past, and gone is gone;"
With looking back afar to see how well
We could have 'scaped our losses, and have won
High fortune. Ever greatest turns on least,
Like Earth's own whirl to atom poles decreased.

LXXV

For in the gloomiest hour a letter came,
Shot arrow–like across the Western sea,
Praising the West; its message was the same
As many a time ere now had languidly
Dropp'd at his feet, but this the rude gale bore
To heart – Gerald will quit our Irish shore.

LXXV

And quit his Love whom he completely loves;
Who loves him just as much? Nay, downcast youth!
Nay, dear mild maiden! – Surely it behooves
That somewhere in the day there should be ruth
For innocent blindness? Lead, on, lead them now
One step, but one! – Their fates do not allow.

LXXVII

The parting scene is brief and frosty dumb.
The unlike sisters stand alike unmoved;
For Milly's soul is wilder'd, weak, and numb,
That reft away which seem'd so dearly proved.
While thought and speech she struggles to recover
Her hand is prest – and he is gone for ever.

LXXVIII

Time speeds: on an October afternoon
Across the well–known view he looks his last;
The valley clothed with peace and fruitful boon,
The chapel where such happy hours were pass'd,
With rainbow–colour'd foliage round its eaves,
And windows all a–glitter through the leaves.

LXXIX

The cottage–smokes, the river; – gaze no more,
Sad heart! although thou canst not, wouldst not shun
The vision future years will oft restore,
Whereon the light of many a summer sun,
The stars of many a winter night shall be
Mingled in one strange sighing memory.

"Under the Abbey Wall"

"Fireside Story"

4
Laurence Bloomfield in Ireland

Allingham's ambitious verse novel was highly popular when it was first seri-
alised in Fraser's Magazine, and it has rarely been out of print ever since.
Today, its "solution" to the Irish Question, a willingly benevolent change of
heart by the landlord class, seems naive, and it has been overtaken by events.
It is also unlikely that a significant readership exists for the verse novel.
However, its vignettes and pastiches, of people, places, events, classes and pre-
cious moments, remain as vivid as the day they were written– and passages like
"The Eviction" and "The Fair" have become precious historical records.
Those passages and others are presented here.

THE EVICTION

In early morning twilight, raw and chill,
Damp vapours brooding on the barren hill,
Through miles of mire in steady grave array
Threescore well–arm'd police pursue their way;
Each tall and bearded man a rifle swings,
And under each greatcoat a bayonet clings:
The Sheriff on his sturdy cob astride
Talks with the chief, who marches by their side,
And, creeping on behind them, Paudeen Dhu
Pretends his needful duty much to rue.
Six big–boned labourers, clad in common freize,
Walk in the midst, the Sheriff's staunch allies;
Six crowbar men, from distant county brought, –
Orange, and glorying in their work, 'tis thought,
But wrongly,– churls of Catholics are they,
And merely hired at half a crown a day.
The hamlet clustering on its hill is seen,
A score of petty homesteads, dark and mean;
Poor always, not despairing until now;
Long used, as well as poverty knows how,
With life's oppressive trifles to contend.

This day will bring its history to an end.
Moveless and grim against the cottage walls
Lean a few silent men: but someone calls
Far off; and then a child 'without a stitch'
Runs out of doors, flies back with piercing screech,
And soon from house to house is heard the cry
Of female sorrow, swelling loud and high,
Which makes the men blaspheme between their teeth.
Meanwhile, o'er fence and watery field beneath,
The little army moves through drizzling rain;
A 'Crowbar' leads the Sheriff's nag; the lane
Is enter'd, and their plashing tramp draws near,
One instant, outcry holds its breath to hear
"Halt!" – at the doors they form in double line,
And ranks of polish'd rifles wetly shine.
The Sheriff's painful duty must be done;
He begs for quiet–and the work's begun.
The strong stand ready; now appear the rest,
Girl, matron, grandsire, baby on the breast,
And Rosy's thin face on a pallet borne;
A motley concourse, feeble and forlorn.
One old man, tears upon his wrinkled cheek,
Stands trembling on a threshold, tries to speak,
But, in defect of any word for this,
Mutely upon the doorpost prints a kiss,
Then passes out for ever. Through the crowd
The children run bewilder'd, wailing loud;
Where needed most, the men combine their aid;
And, last of all, is Oona forth convey'd,
Reclined in her accustom'd strawen chair,
Her aged eyelids closed, her thick white hair
Escaping from her cap; she feels the chill,
Looks round and murmurs, then again is still.
Now bring the remnants of each household fire;
On the wet ground the hissing coals expire;
And Paudeen Dhu, with meekly dismal face,
Receives the full possession of the place.

THE FAIR

Ere yet the sun has dried on hedge and furze
Their silver veils of dewy gossamers,
Along the winding road to Lisnamoy
The drover trudges and the country boy,
With cows that fain would crop its fringe of sward,
And pigs, their hindfoot jerking in a cord,
And bleating sheep; the farmer jogs his way,
Or plies his staff and legs of woollen gray;
The basket–bearing goodwives slowly move,
White–capt, with colour'd kerchief tied above,
On foot, or in the cart–front placed on high
To jolt along in lumbering luxury;
Men, women, pigs, cows, sheep, and horses tend
One way, and to the Harvest Fair they wend;
Jack Doran with the rest, with sorry cheer,
Condemn'd at Pigot's Office to appear, –
To him a place of awe, and doubt, and fear.

'Tis where the road–side rivulet expands,
And every–stone upon its image stands,
The country maidens finish their attire,
Screen'd by the network of a tangled briar;
On grassy bank their shapely limbs indue
With milk–white stockings and the well–black'd shoe,
And court that mirror for a final grace,

The dazzling ribbons nodding round their face.
Behold our Bridget tripping to the fair;
Her shawl is splendid, but her feet are bare;
Till, quick the little bundle here untied,
The shoes come forth, the skirts are shaken wide,
And Biddy enters Lisnamoy in pride;

AGRICULTURE

It that it be the old or newborn day.
Alas! the year has touched its height of hope.
And lessening day on day begin to slope
To gloomy winter. All we know, must die;
But when we feel it , who forbears to sigh?–
To bed, to bed! Amidst the doubtful gleam;
And mingle past and future in a dream.

Says Downing, brought by Bloomfield round the land
Next morning,– Now at last I understand.
"I knew your liberal notions, never knew
"How you contrived to raise your rental too.
"I see you have as groundwork, study made,
"Close, persevering, of the farmer's trade.
"Hard work, no doubt, at first."
"Plans fail'd beside,
"And many cheated, more to cheat me tried;
"All has work'd round by slow and sure degree,
"To something doubtless, – but one never sees
"His hope come true; in daylight disappear
"The vision's glories.......Let me show you here
"A solid thing enough. Seven years ago
"With gorse above, and plashy bog below,
"This was a dreary wilderness and wide,
"With one poor cottage on the moorland–side.
"Twelve little households now possess a place,
"And each the centre of a widening space
"Of useful ground. Besides their work at home,
"The men and youths to farming labour come
"In Spring or Harvest on the neighbouring lands,
"But not as once with slavish hungry hands,
"Toiling for husks, and as they toil'd the more,
"More helpless, pinch'd, and poorer than before."
– "Wages are higher?" – "Yes I gladly say,
"And far more work too finish'd in a day.
"Every day–labourer, if worthy found,
"Ere long obtains a cheap small bit of ground;
"Help with a house; with more ambitious eyes,
"May look to win a waste–plot if he tries;

"But first probationary powers must show,
"And on the list with all his rivals go.
"There shoul be, as the soldiers have in France,
"In humblest work an opening to advance.
"Best government gives every man his chance.
"That's justice, – but still more the weak may claim,
"And merely justice in the strong to blame."

IRISH TRAVELLERS

Who shouting gallops, leg on either side
Grazing the ground his head behind is shorn,
Thin curls the lean and cunning cheek adorn;
Short coat of frieze, cord breeches to the knee,
A low–crown'd hat, a shirt–neck flying free,
His tribe a partner yields; his donkey bears
At need his children, furniture and wears;
Donkeys at many a fair he buys and sells,
And here among his like, swears loud and yells.
Beyond them are the horses; there, sweet kine;
There, flocks of sheep; there, fulsome–smelling swine.

THE WORKHOUSE

Inn, fountain, clock, we pass, and quit the town
Close by the Workhouse, where with Isaac Brown
Hath Bloomfield many a tedious battle fought,
And many a good reform full slowly wrought;
For weekly there, sat once a Guardian Board
To guard the landlord's purse from pauper horde,
To guard the bed where age and sickness lie
From touch of comfort – let them live or die, –
What matter how their drop of life runs by?
To guard poor children trembling little slaves,
Cast on our pity by misfortune's waves,
From spade and neddle, watching lest they learn
The skill that might a scantest living earn,
Using faith, faith, hope and charity being dead,
Political economy instead,
Training with anxious negligence a race
To live their country's burden and disgrace.
Sad without guilt, and punish'd without crime,
Those joyless children dragg'd their weary time,
Or issuing from their prison two by two
Distress'd the road with cheeks of ghastly hue, –
Unlike the brisk though tatter'd urchins there,
Not highly fed, but free from Guardians' care.

THE DORANS

Jack Doran's cottage, from a bare hillside,
Looks out across the bogland black and wide,
Where some few ridges broke the swarthy soil,
A patch of culture, won with patient toil;
The walls were mud, around an earthen floor,
Straw ropes held on the thatch, and by his door
A screen of wattles fenced the wind away,
For open wide from morn till dusk it lay,
A stool perhaps across, for barring out
The too familiar porker's greedy snout;
Thieves were undreamt of, vagrants not repell'd,
A gift of five potatoes, gently given,
Or fist of meal, repaid with hopes of Heaven.

There Jack and Maureen, Neal their only son,
And daughter Bridget, saw the seasons run;
Poor but contented peasants, warm and kind,
Of hearty manners, and religious mind;
Busy to make their little corner good,
And full of health, upon the homeliest food.
They tasted flesh–meat hardly thrice a year,
Crock–butter, when the times were not too dear,
Salt herring as a treat, as luxury
For Sunday mornings and cold weather, tea;
Content they were if mild the noggins crown'd,
What time their oatmeal–stirabout went round,
Or large potatoes, teeming from the pit, –
Milk of its precious butter duly stript,
Wherewith to Lisnamoy young Biddy tript.
Not poor they seem'd to neighbours poorer still,
As Doran's father was, ere bog and hill
Gave something for his frugal fight of years
'Gainst marsh and rock, and furze with all its spears,
And round the cottage an oasis green
Amidst the dreary wilderness was seen.
Two hardy cows the pail and churn supplied,
Short–leg'd, big–boned, with rugged horns and wide,
That each good spot among the heather knew,
And every blade that by the runnels grew,

Roved on the moor at large, but meekly came
With burden'd udders to delight the dame,
And in its turn the hoarded stocking swell'd
Which envious neighbours in their dreams beheld;
At thought whereof were bumpkins fain to cast
Sheep's eyes at comely Bridget as she pass'd
With napkin–shaped basket many a morn;
But every bumpkin Bridget laugh'd to scorn.

WEDDED LOVE

O happy Husband! – happy Wife no less!
In perfect mutual trust and tenderness.
Whatever joys await the Blest above,
No boon below like happy wedded love.

DOWNING

Voice of Bloomfield:

"No burglar reconnoitres your abode.
"No footpad dogs you on the lonely road,
"No ruffian's arm or cowardly parotte,
"Walk where you please, is flung across your throat;
"No pistol – pointing mask, with stealthy light,
"Across your slumber stoops at dead of night;
"No friendly neighbour, spouse, or next of kin,
"Mixes your glass, to drop the powder in;
"Confess, when you have search'd the wide world round,
"You're nowhere safer than on Irish ground.
"We Paddies, Downing, you must understand,
"Count England as a dangerous heathen land!"
– "I own, though we of Irish things complain
"Your native manners are of gentler strain.

NEWSPAPERS

Hot grew men's passions: golden harvest came
And ended: hotter wax'd this evil flame,
Turning all wholesome thoughts to dread and hate.
Jack to his own fireside kept close of late,
But Neal was not afraid to cross their hill
To Ballytullagh, welcomed with good–will,
When nightfall shadow'd mountain, moor, and glen,
To chat the girls and argue with the men,
Or study in the 'Firebrand's, Dublin print,
Seditious rhetoric and murderous hint.

"The Boy's Grave"

5

THE BUBBLE

See, the pretty Planet!
Floating sphere!
Faintest breeze will fan it
Far or near;

World as light as feather;
Moonshine rays,
Rainbow tints, together,
As it plays;

Drooping, sinking, failing,
Nigh to earth,
Mounting, whirling, sailing,
Full of mirth;

Life there, welling, flowing,
Waving round;
Pictures coming, going,
Without sound.

Quick now! Be this airy
Globe repell'd!
Never can the fairy
Star be held.

Touch'd – it in a twinkle
Disappears!
Leaving but a sprinkle,
As of tears.

THE TOUCHSTONE

A man there came, whence none could tell,
Bearing a Touchstone in his hand;
And tested all things in the land
By its unerring spell.

Quick birth of transmutation smote
The fair to foul, the foul to fair;
Purple nor ermine did he spare,
Nor scorn the dusty coat.

Of heirloom jewels, prized so much,
Were many changed to chips and clods,
And even statues of the Gods
Crumbled beneath its touch.

Then angrily the people cried,
"The loss outweighs the profit far;
Our goods suffice us as they are
We will not have them tried."

And since they could not so prevail
To check this unrelenting guest,
They seized him, saying – "Let him test
How real it is, our jail!"

But, though they slew him with the sword,
And in a fire his Touchstone burn'd,
Its doings could not be o'erturned,
Its undoings restored.

And when to stop all future harm,
They strew'd its ashes on the breeze;
They little guess'd each grain of these
Convey'd the perfect charm.

North, south, in rings and amulets,
Throughout the crowded world 'tis borne;
Which, as a fashion long outworn,
In ancient mind forgets.

THE WINDING BANKS OF ERNE

Adieu to Belashanny !
where I was bred and born;
Go where I may, I'll think of you,
as sure as night and morn.
The kindly spot, the friendly town,
where every one is known,
And not a face in all the place
but partly seems my own;
There's not a house or window,
there's not a field or hill,
But, east or west, in foreign lands,
I'll recollect them still.
I leave my warm heart with you,
tho' my back I'm forced to turn—
Adieu to Belashanny,
and the winding banks of Erne!

No more on pleasant evenings
we'll saunter down the Mall,
When the trout is rising to the fly,
the salmon to the fall.
The boat comes straining on her net,
and heavily she creeps,
Cast on, cast off—she feels the oars,
and to her berth she sweeps;
Now fore and aft keep hauling,
and gathering up the clew,
Till a silver wave of salmon
rolls in among the crew.
Then they may sit, with pipes a–lit,
and many a joke and 'yarn';—
Adieu to Belashanny,
and the winding banks of Erne!

The music of the waterfall,
the mirror of the tide,
When all the green–hill'd harbour
is full from side to side,
From Portnasun to Bulliebawns,

and round the Abbey Bay,
From rocky Inis Saimer
to Coolnargit sandhills gray;
While far upon the southern line,
to guard it like a wall,
The Leitrim mountains clothed in blue
gaze calmly over all,
And watch the ship sail up or down,
the red flag at her stern;—
Adieu to these, adieu to all
the winding banks of Erne!

Farewell to you, Kildoney lads,
and them that pull an oar,
A lug–sail set, or haul a net,
from the Point to Mullaghmore;
From Killybegs to bold Slieve–League,
that ocean–mountain steep,
Six hundred yards in air aloft,
six hundred in the deep,:
From Dooran to the Fairy Bridge,
and round by Tullen strand,
Level and long, and white with waves,
where gull and curlew stand;
Head out to sea when on your lee
the breakers you discern!—
Adieu to all the billowy coast,
and winding banks of Erne!

Farewell, Coolmore,—Bundoran ! and
your summer crowds that run
From inland homes to see with joy
th' Atlantic–setting sun;
To breathe the buoyant salted air,
and sport among the waves;
To gather shells on sandy beach,
and tempt the gloomy caves;
To watch the flowing, ebbing tide,
the boats, the crabs, the fish;
Young men and maids to meet and smile,

"Window"

and form a tender wish;
The sick and old in search of health,
for all things have their turn—
And I must quit my native shore,
and the winding banks of Erne!

Farewell to every white cascade
from the Harbour to Belleek,
And every pool where fins may rest,
and ivy–shaded creek;
The sloping fields, the lofty rocks,.
where ash and holly grow,
The one split yew–tree gazing
on the curving flood below;
The Lough, that winds through islands
under Turaw mountain green;
And Castle Caldwell's stretching woods,
with tranquil bays between;

And Breesie Hill, and many a pond
among the heath and fern,—
For I must say adieu—adieu
to the winding banks of Erne!

The thrush will call through Camlin groves
the live–long summer day;
The waters run by mossy cliff,
and banks with wild flowers gay;
The girls will bring their work and sing
beneath a twisted thorn,
Or stray with sweethearts down the path
among the growing corn;
Along the river–side they go,
where I have often been,
Oh, never shall I see again
the happy days I've seen!
A thousand chances are to one
I never may return,—
Adieu to Belashanny;
and the winding banks of Erne!

Adieu to evening dances,
when merry neighbours meet,
And the fiddle says to boys and girls,
'Get up and shake your feet!'
To 'seanachas' and wise old talk
of Erin's days gone by—

Who trench'd the rath on such a hill,
and where the bones–may lie
Of saint, or king, or warrior chief;
with tales of fairy power,
And tender ditties sweetly sung
to pass the twilight hour.
The mournful song of exile
is now for me to learn—
Adieu, my dear companions
on the winding banks of Erne!

Now measure from the Commons down
to each end of the Purt,
Round the Abbey, Moy, and Knather,—
I wish no one any hurt;
The Main Street, Back Street, College Lane,
the Mall, and Portnasun,
If any foes of mine are there,
I pardon every one.
I hope that man and womankind
will do the same by me;
For my heart is sore and heavy
at voyaging the sea.
My loving friends I'll bear in mind,
and often fondly turn
To think of Belashanny,
and the winding banks of Erne.

If ever I'm a money'd man,
I mean, please God, to cast
My golden anchor in the place
where youthful years were pass'd;
Though heads that now are black and brown
must meanwhile gather gray,

New faces rise by every hearth,
and old ones drop away—
Yet dearer still that Irish hill
than all the world beside;
It's home, sweet home, where'er I roam
through lands and waters wide.
And if the Lord allows me,
I surely will return
To my native Belashanny,
and the winding banks of Erne.

AN EVENING.

A sunset's mounded cloud
A diamond evening–star
Sad blue hills afar;
Love in his shroud.

Scarcely a tear to shed;
Hardly a word to say;
The end of a summer day;
Sweet Love dead.

IN SNOW

O English mother, in the ruddy glow
Hugging your baby closer when outside
You see the silent, soft, and cruel snow
Falling again, and think what ills betide
Unshelter'd creatures,–your sad thoughts may go
Where War and Winter now, two spectre–wolves,
Hunt in the freezing vapour that involves
Those Asian peaks of ice and gulfs below.
Does this young Soldier heed the snow that fills
His mouth and open eyes? or mind, in truth,
To–night, his mother's parting syllables?
Ha! is't a red coat?–Merely blood. Keep ruth
For others; this is but an Afghan youth
Shot by the stranger on his native hills.

PLACES AND MEN

In Sussex here, by shingle and by sand,
Flat fields and farmsteads in their wind–blown trees,
The shallow tide–wave courses to the land,
And all along the down a fringe one sees
Of ducal woods. That 'dim discovered spire'
Is Chichester, where Collins felt a fire
Touch his sad lips; thatched Felpham roofs are these,
Where happy Blake found heaven more close at hand.
Goodwood and Arundel possess their lords,
Successive in the towers and groves, which stay;
These two poor men, by some right of their own,
Possessed the earth and sea, the sun and moon,
The inner sweet of life; and put in words
A personal force that doth not pass away.

A SINGER

That which he did not feel, he would not sing;
What most he felt, religion it was to hide
In a dumb darkling grotto, where the spring
Of tremulous tears, arising unespied,
Became a holy well that durst not glide
Into the day with moil or murmuring;
Whereto, as if to some unlawful thing,
He stole, musing or praying at its side.
But in the sun he sang with cheerful heart,
Of coloured season and the whirling sphere,
Warm household habitude and human mirth,
The whole faith–blooded mystery of earth;
And I, who had his secret, still could hear
The grotto's whisper low through every part.

IN A SPRING GROVE

Here the white–ray'd anemone is born,
Wood–sorrel, and the varnish'd buttercup;
And primrose in its purfled green swathed up,
Pallid and sweet round every budding thorn,
Gray ash, and beech with rusty leaves outworn.
Here, too the darting linnet hath her nest
In the blue–lustred holly, never shorn,
Whose partner cheers her little brooding breast,
Piping from some near bough. O simple song!
O cistern deep of that harmonious rillet,
And these fair juicy stems that climb and throng
The vernal world, and unexhausted seas
Of flowing life, and soul that asks to fill it,
Each and all of these,–and more, and more than these!

THE LITTLE DELL

Doleful was the land,
Dull on, every side,
Neither soft n'or grand,
Barren, bleak, and wide;
Nothing look'd with love;
All was dingy brown;
The very skies above
Seem'd to sulk and frown.

Plodding sick and sad,
Weary day on day;
Searching, never glad,
Many a miry way;
Poor existence lagg'd
In this barren place;
While the seasons dragg'd
Slowly o'er its face.

Spring, to sky and ground,
Came before I guess'd;
Then one day I found
A valley, like a nest!
Guarded with a spell
Sure it must have been,
This little fairy dell
Which I had never seen.

Open to the blue,
Green banks hemm'd it round
A rillet wander'd through
With a tinkling sound;
Briars among the rocks
Tangled arbours made;
Primroses in flocks
Grew beneath their shade.

Merry birds a few,
Creatures wildly tame,
Perch'd and sung and flew;
Timid field–mice came;
Beetles in the moss
Journey'd here and there;
Butterflies across
Danced through sunlit air.

There I often read,
Sung alone, or dream'd;
Blossoms overhead,
Where the west wind stream'd;
Small horizon–line,
Smoothly lifted up,
Held this world of mine
In a grassy cup.

The barren land to-day
Hears my last adieu:
Not an hour I stay;
Earth is wide and new.
Yet, farewell, farewell!
May the sun and show'rs
Bless that Little Dell.

THE BOY

The Boy from his bedroom–window
Look'd over the little town,
And away to the bleak black upland
Under a clouded moon.

The moon came forth from her cavern,
He saw the sudden gleam
Of a tarn in the swarthy moorland;
Or perhaps the whole was a dream.

For I never could find that water
In all my walks and rides:
Far–off, in the Land of Memory,
That midnight pool abides.

Many fine things had I glimpse of,
And said, "I shall find them one day."
Whether within or without me
They were, I cannot say.

A GRAVESTONE

Far from the churchyard dig his grave,
On some green mound beside the wave;
To westward, sea and sky alone,
And sunsets. Put a mossy stone,
With mortal name and date, a harp
And bunch of wild flowers, carven sharp;
Then leave it free to winds that blow,
And patient mosses creeping; slow,
And wandering wings, and footsteps rare
Of human creature pausing there.

HALF-WAKING

I thought it was the little bed
I slept in long ago;
A straight white curtain at the head,
And two smooth knobs below.
I thought I saw the nursery fire,
And in a chair well–known
My mother sat, and did not tire
With reading all alone.
If I should make the slightest sound
To show that I'm awake,
She'd rise, and lap the blankets round,
My pillow softly shake;
Kiss me, and turn my face to see
The shadows on the wall,
And then sing Rousseau's Dream to me,
Till fast asleep I fall.
But this is not my little bed;
That time is far away;
With strangers now I live instead,
From dreary day to day.

THE FAIRIES

Up the airy mountain,
Down the rushy glen,
We daren't go a–hunting
For fear of little men;
Wee folk, good folk,
Trooping all together;
Green jacket, red cap,
And white owl's feather!
Down along the rocky shore
Some make their home,
They live on crispy pancakes
Of yellow tide–foam;
Some in the reeds
Of the black mountain lake,
With frogs for their watch–dogs,
All night awake.

High on the hill–top
The old King sits;
He is now so old and gray
He's nigh lost his wits.
With a bridge of white mist
Columbkill he crosses,
On his stately journeys
From Slieveleague to Rosses;
Or going up with music
On cold starry nights,
To sup with the Queen
Of the gay Northern Lights.

They stole little Bridget
For seven years long;
When she came down again
Her friends were all gone.
They took her lightly back,
Between the night and morrow,
They thought that she was fast asleep,
But she was dead with sorrow.
They have kept her ever since
Deep within the lake,
On a bed of flag–leaves,
Watching till she wake.

By the craggy hill–side,
Through the mosses bare,
They have planted thorn–trees
For pleasure here and there.
Is any man so daring
As dig them up in spite,
He shall find their sharpest thorns
In his bed at night.

Up the airy mountain,
Down the rushy glen,
We daren't go a–hunting
For fear of little men;
Wee folk, good folk,
Trooping all together;
Green jacket, red cap,
And white owl's feather

omhairie Chonta
Átha Cliath Theas

Index of first lines

Index by title

Also Available from Voice Books

Drumboe Woods, the ecology and history of an Irish woodland.

www.voicebooks.net